Macramé Jewelry

Step-by-Step Instructions for Stylish Designs

Diana Crialesi

Dover Publications, Inc.
Mineola, New York

Bibliographical Note

This Dover edition, first published in 2018, is an unabridged
republication of the English translation of the work originally
published by Snake SA, Switzerland, in 2016.

International Standard Book Number
ISBN-13: 978-0-486-82376-8
ISBN-10: 0-486-82376-8

Manufactured in the United States by LSC Communications
82376801   2018
www.doverpublications.com

Macramé
Jewelry

Introduction

The term *macramé* probably derives from the Arabic word *mahrama*, meaning "handkerchief"; in Turkish, *makramà* means a towel or an embroidered headscarf. Macramé is also known as "knotted lace": the technique involves making knots on a series of vertical cords, plaited and knotted by hand, without resorting to knitting needles or crochet hooks. The geometrical motifs that are produced can be decorated with fringed borders.

Fringes and knots are the distinctive traits of this very ancient technique, creating ornaments of various kinds: it seems that as early as 3000 B.C. Sumerians used this technique for closing off fabric edges. Macramé probably reached Italy during the fifteenth century, a period characterized by intense mercantile activities; during their long hours at sea, sailors made hammocks, belts, handbags and other macramé objects by knotting cords made of string using this technique—in fact, some of the knots are similar to those used in sailing. Italian women, beginning with those from the Liguria region, refined this technique thanks to the use of thinner thread, therefore producing objects in delicate lace. Macramé was further developed during the seventeenth and eighteenth centuries; in households, convents and monasteries it was used to decorate towels, sheets and household linen and as part of bridal dowries and ecclesiastical furnishings. With the onset of emigration, this technique began to spread, especially to South America. A traditional family legacy, from one generation to the next macramé assumed various aspects depending upon the flair and skills of its creators, but always remaining true to its basic motifs.

Contents

2 Introduction

4 Contents

6 Materials and tools

8 Primary knots and hitching

20 Wrap-around spiral

24 Knots and strings of light

30 Geometries and contrasts

36 Leaf magic

42 Leaf-shaped earrings

46 A thousand blue waves

50 Wave-shaped earrings

54 Donut bracelet

58 Infinity waves

64 Drop earrings

72 Ethnic earrings

78 Ethnic cabochon

Materials and tools

Use a flat, rigid surface that guarantees stability: the best option would be a macramé board, which is fitted with grooves on the sides that help to block the strings. You will also need strings and twine of various thicknesses (from cotton thread to braided rat-tail) in a variety of colors; measuring tape; electric thread zap tool; scissors; tapestry needle; beads and crystals of various colors, shapes and sizes; perhaps a few beads of polymer clay (in the shape of the original "donut"); link chains; clasps; working cord; snap-hooks; and connecting rings in metal.

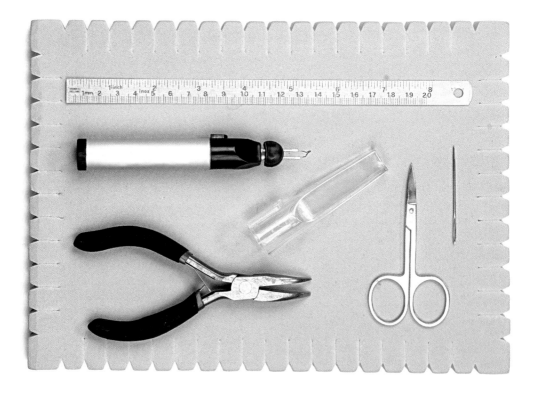

Primary knots and hitching

In order to make knots properly, you must make a distinction between the different strings used and understand their purpose. The holding cord (see box on page 15) acts as support, while the knotting cord, the one knotted to the holding cord, is used to make the knots themselves. During the process, these strings may even exchange their roles: the holding cord may become the knotting cord and vice-versa.

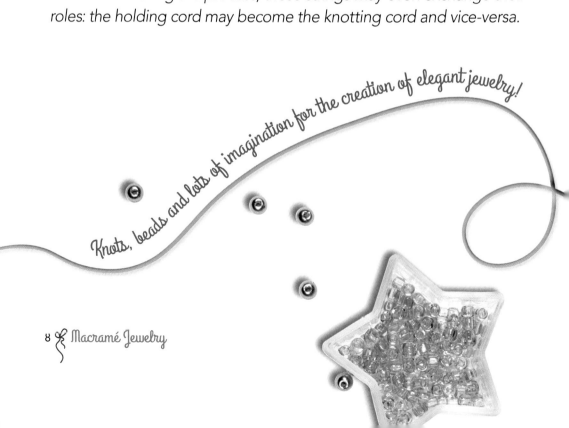

Knots, beads and lots of imagination for the creation of elegant jewelry!

Lark's head knot

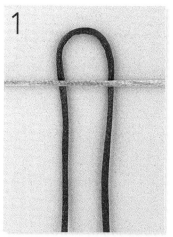

1 • Secure the holding cord to the board. Fold the string, creating an upside-down loop. Insert this loop under the holding cord.

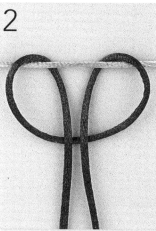

2 • Pull the length of the strings through the loop, over the holding cord.

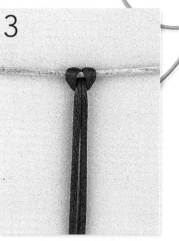

3 • Pull the ends downward to snug, or secure, the knot.

Overhand knot

1 • Make a loop.

2 • Bring the end of the string behind the loop and through the loop.

3 • Pull the ends to snug the knot.

Half knot

1 • Secure the holding cord to the board. Pass the knotting cord over the holding cord, then underneath the holding cord and over the other end of the knotting cord itself.

2 • Repeat step 1.

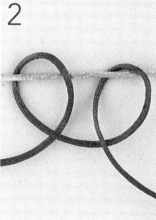

3 • Pull the ends to snug the knot.

Berry knot

This is a sequence of primary knots on various strings worked vertically.

1 • Hitch the strings next to each other on the holding cord using knots or other methods. Take the first knotting cord, on the left, and hitch it snugly to the right.

2 • Take the second string on the left and pass it over the holding cord (from bottom to top), through the loop and pull snugly.

3 • Repeat and pull snugly. The first primary knot is done.

4 • Make a primary knot with all the strings, going left to right. The result is a design that may be horizontal, vertical or diagonal, depending on how it is secured to the holding cord. The same design can even be done from right to left.

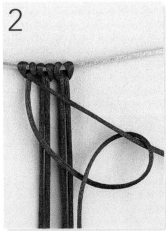

Half square knot

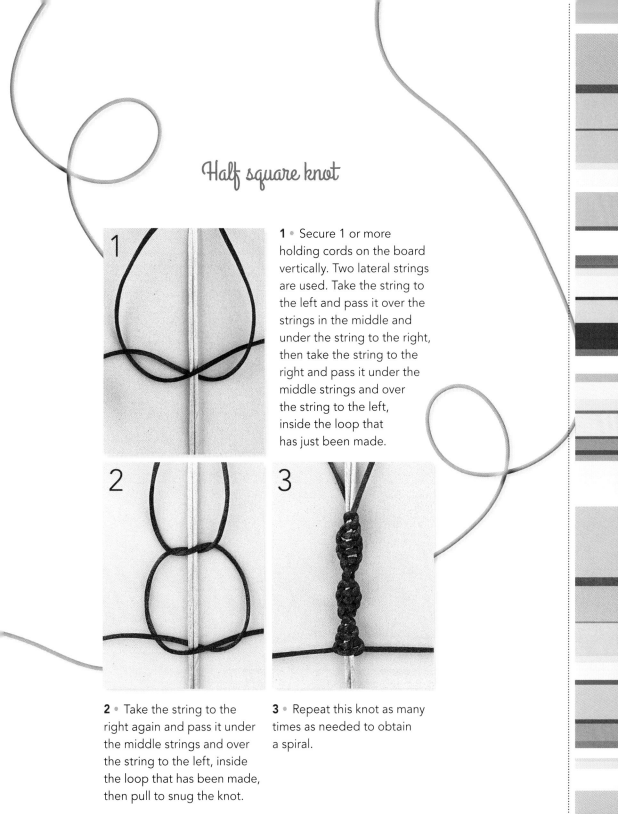

1 • Secure 1 or more holding cords on the board vertically. Two lateral strings are used. Take the string to the left and pass it over the strings in the middle and under the string to the right, then take the string to the right and pass it under the middle strings and over the string to the left, inside the loop that has just been made.

2 • Take the string to the right again and pass it under the middle strings and over the string to the left, inside the loop that has been made, then pull to snug the knot.

3 • Repeat this knot as many times as needed to obtain a spiral.

Square knot

1 • Secure 1 or more holding cords to the board vertically. Use the 2 lateral strings. Take the string to the left and pass it under the middle strings and over the string to the right. Take the string to the right and pass it over the middle strings and under the string to the left, inside the loop that has been made.

2 • Take the string to the left and pass it over the middle strings and under the string to the right.

3 • Take the string to the right and pass it under the middle strings and over the string to the left, inside the loop that has been made, then pull to snug the knot.

4 • With a sequence of square knots you can make an adjustable fastening for bracelets (such as the one called "Geometries and contrasts," for example).

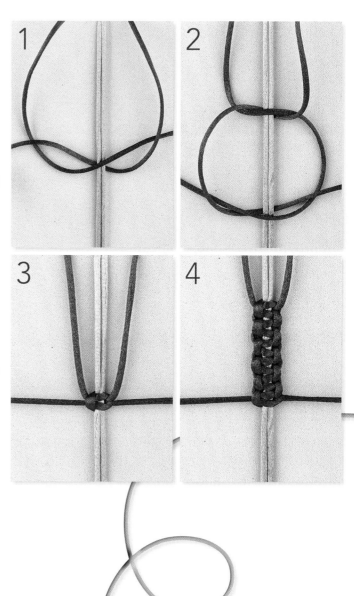

Loop

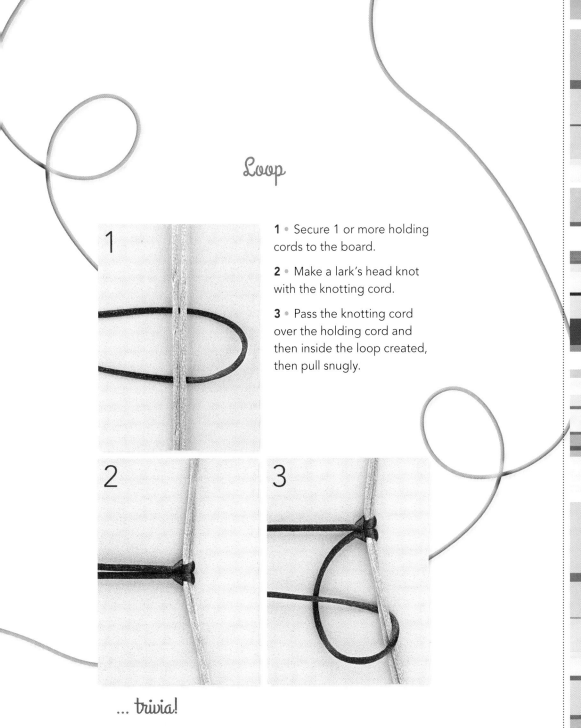

1 • Secure 1 or more holding cords to the board.

2 • Make a lark's head knot with the knotting cord.

3 • Pass the knotting cord over the holding cord and then inside the loop created, then pull snugly.

... trivia!

The "holding cord" is the one acting as an anchor for all the other knots about to be made. It must be securely fixed to the board either horizontally or vertically so that it is stretched perfectly taut.

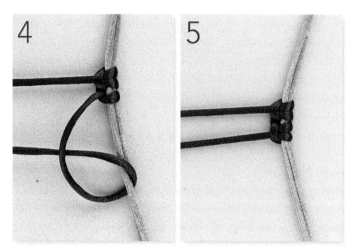

4 - 5 • Pass the knotting cord under the holding cord and then inside the loop that has just been made, then pull to snug the knot.

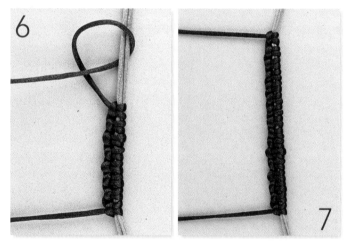

6 - 7 • Repeat this knot a desired number of times to the right of the middle knot and then the same number of times to the left (the number varies, depending on the dimension of the loop you wish to create). For the patterns in this book, make 9 knots on one side and then 9 knots on the other.

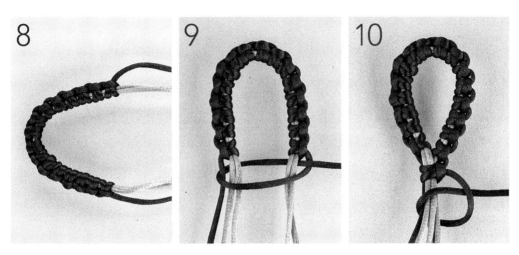

8 - 9 - 10 - 11 • Make a loop and close it with the same type of knot just made, gathering all the strings and repeating the knot 2 times or more. The loop is ready.

Difficulty levels

Each one of the macramé objects in this volume has a specific difficulty level. These symbols will help you identify these levels and decide which model to try your hand at.

▶ **Easy**

▶ **Easy-medium**

▶ **Intermediate**

▶ **Challenging**

Wrap-around spiral

An easy-to-make and trendy bracelet, to be wrapped around the wrist twice. It can also be used as a simple and very colorful necklace.

Material needed for the bracelet

▶ Salmon macramé twine, .8mm thick

▶ Beads in colored polymer clay in different shapes, with threading holes of at least 2mm in diameter

Cut 2 strings equal to $86^2/_3$ in. in length. Fold in half and make a loop as explained in the tutorial on page 15. The bracelet will be made entirely with half square knots.

1 • Insert 1 holding cord into the loop and secure it to the macramé board, thus dividing the strings by securing 2 to the middle and knotting the other 2.

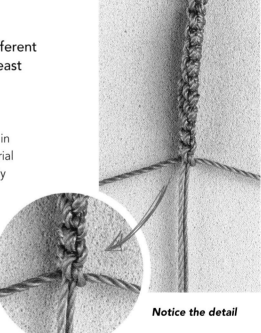

Notice the detail

2 • Using the 2 side strings, make a half square knot on the two middle strings, then another half square knot using the same method.

3 • Make a series of half square knots. As you knot, a spiral will be formed and the strings will change their position approximately every 4–5 knots. Continue until the piece measures approximately $1^3/_{16}$ in. in length.

Thread 1 bead through the
4 • 2 central strings and knot the other 2 by crossing over the bead sideways.

Notice the detail

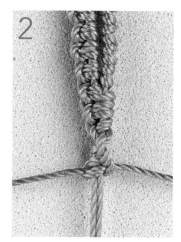

You can even use large beads made of glass or ceramics

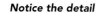

(... warning!

When you notice the strings exchanging places, then pass the string on the left to the right and vice-versa.

5 • Continue by making more half square knots underneath the bead, in the same manner.

6 • Repeat the sequence made with 1³/₁₆ in. of knots plus bead until the middle of the bracelet. This pattern goes twice around the wrist, so stop when you reach a length equal to once around the wrist, which on the average is equal to 12²/₃–14¹/₁₆ in.

7 • Invert the position of the strings: the two strings that were previously knotted should not go through the bead and they should be secured at the bottom of the board. Continue with the other 2 strings in the 1³/₁₆ in. knotting plus bead sequence, until you reach a length of 12²/₃–14¹/₁₆ in. Tie all 4 strings together.

8 • Burn the ends of 2 strings and thread the other 2 strings through a bead that has the right size to accommodate both of them and is big enough to be blocked inside the top loop, then make 1 knot underneath the bead. Cut and burn the ends of the strings. The bracelet is now complete.

Knots and strings of light

A spectacular bracelet that can be used in so
many ways: to change its style and transform it into a different
accessory time and time again, all you have to do is change
the form and color of its beads.

Material needed for the bracelet

▶ Orange
macramé twine,
.5mm thick

▶ Orange
11/0 seed beads

▶ Glass beads in different shapes and
colors (tubular, seed beads 8/0, seed
beads 11/0, cubic) in green, orange,
purple, gold and red

▶ Orange ring-shaped crystals,
3 x 4mm

▶ Gold-colored drop-shaped
fastening bead, ¹/₂ x ¹/₃ in.

... some advice

*You can use beads of every
shape, color and size to
make the bracelet more
dynamic and entertaining.*

Cut 3 strings with a length of 47¼ in. and 1 string with a length of 63 in. Fold in half and make a loop as explained in the tutorial on page 15.

1 • Insert 1 holding cord into the loop and secure it to the macramé board, then fan all the strings out towards the bottom. Take 1 string and secure it horizontally to the left. This will be your holding cord.

Notice the detail

2 • Take the first string to the right and make 1 half knot on the holding cord. Continue the same way with the third, fourth, fifth, sixth and seventh strings, proceeding from right to left.

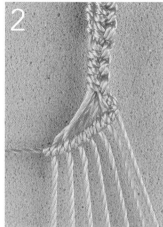

3 • Place the holding cord horizontally to the right. Take the second string to the left and knot it on the holding cord.

4 • Knot all the other strings on the holding cord, going from left to right.

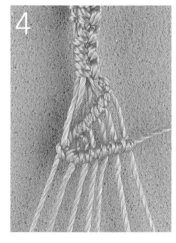

5 • Place the holding cord horizontally to the left. Take the second string to the right and knot it on the holding cord. Knot all the other strings on the holding cord, going from right to left.

6 • Continue this way until you have 6 rows of knots.

7 • Thread some beads through all of the 8 strings or only on 4 of them, depending upon how full you want the bracelet to be. Assess the length depending upon the size of your wrist, keeping in mind that the other end of the bracelet will have another 8 rows of knots.

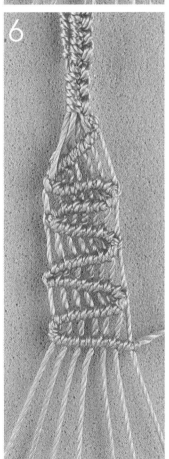

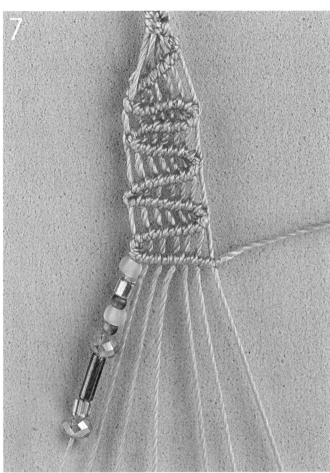

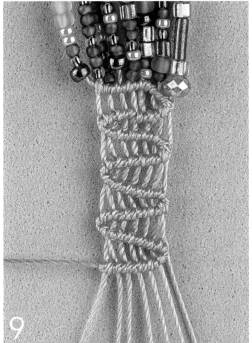

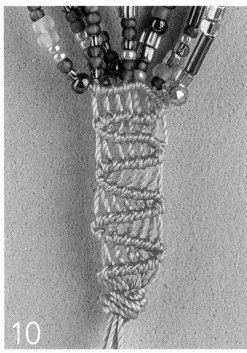

8 • Take the last string on the left, knot it together with the one immediately to its right and secure the string horizontally to the right. Knot all the other strings onto the holding cord, going from left to right.

9 • Continue this way until you have another 7 rows of knots.

10 • Make 1 slipknot using all 8 strings.

11 • Thread 2 strings through 1 bead large enough to block the loop. Knot the 2 strings together and burn the ends. Cut remaining strings 1³⁄₁₆ inches from the knot, thread 1 bead through the end of each, make 1 knot to hold it in place, then burn the ends. Cut remaining strings 1³⁄₁₆ inches from the knot, insert 1 crystal at the end of each, make 1 knot to hold it in place, then burn the end. Thread the bead through the loop to close. The bracelet is now complete.

difficulty

Geometries and contrasts

The charm of this bracelet lies entirely in the contrasts of color and the choice of strings, in the skillful play between thickness and shine. An accessory to be worn day in and day out – with extreme nonchalance.

Material needed for the bracelet

▶ Turquoise macramé twine, .5mm thick

▶ Purple synthetic macramé twine, .5mm thick

▶ 2 crystals or beads of your choice for the fastening

... some advice

You can try your hand at making this simple and basic model even using thicker strings: the final effect will be "fuller" and compact, with your wrist all gussied up!

1 • Cut 12 turquoise strings with a length of 31½ in. and 1 purple string with a length of 3⅕ feet. Secure the 12 strings to the macramé board.

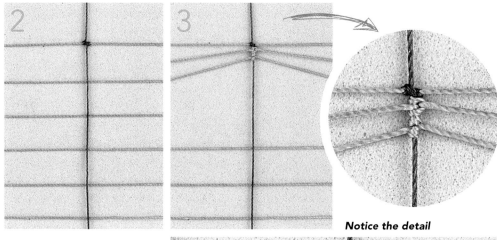

Notice the detail

2 • Arrange the purple string (or of a contrasting color) perpendicularly in the middle and knot it with 1 half knot on the first of the 12 strings.

3 • Knot the following turquoise strings using 1 half knot.

4 • Continue, one string at a time, to make the half knots closer on the holding cord: 2 opposite fans will be created.

5 • Take the purple string (or a contrasting color) and knot it on each of the 12 strings to one side of the fan of your choice, in this case on the right side.

6 • Complete the row of knots.

7 • Work on the first half of the bracelet. Turn the macramé board by 90°, as shown in the photo. Take the right end of the purple string (now the holding cord) and stretch it horizontally to the left.

8 • Knot all the other strings on the holding cord, going from right to left.

9 • Secure the holding cord tautly in a horizontal position to the right. Knot all the other strings on the holding cord, going from left to right.

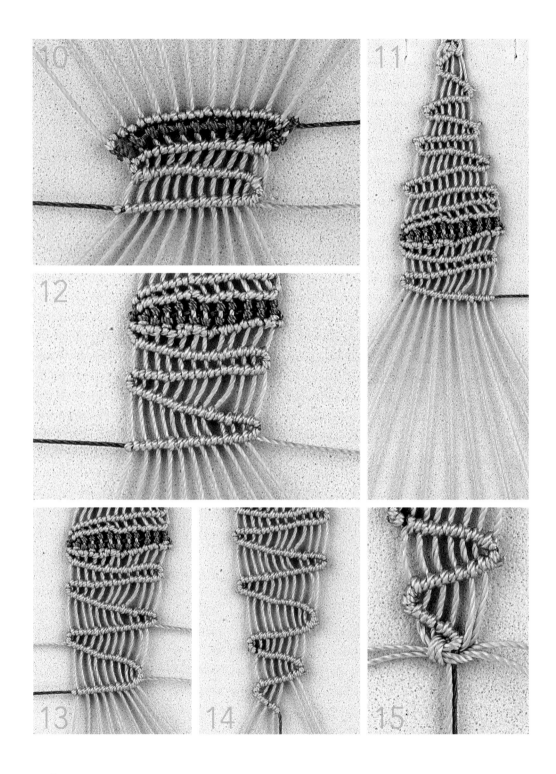

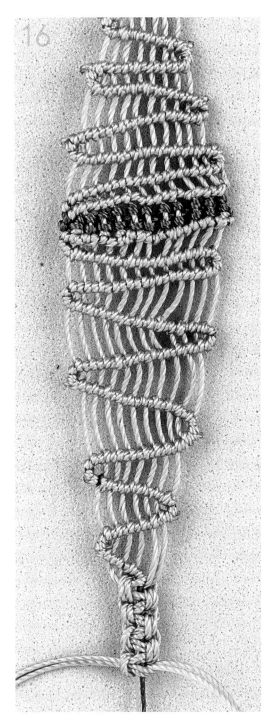

10 • Repeat the same procedure worked previously, from right to left. This will produce another u-bend.

11 • The same procedure should be done on both sides of the central part in purple: now you will see how it proceeds on the second side.

12 • After the third row of knots, block one of the 12 strings horizontally on the macramé board and continue with the other 11 strings. Continue working on the bend, deducting the number of knotted strings at every bend. Each time some strings are deducted, cut and burn the ends that stick out.

13 • Continue by creating a number of bends sufficient to cover more or less half of your wrist.

14 • When, by continuing the deducting process, 5 strings are left plus the holding cord, the time has come to close off the bracelet. Divide strings into 3 groups of 2 each.

15 • Make a sequence of square knots with the couples of strings thus subdivided, knotting the two lateral pairs on the central pair.

16 • After initial 3 square knots, overlap 2 central strings to both sides of the bracelet, closing to form a circle. Make more square knots until reaching wrist measurement. Cut two central strings of same size, make 1 knot, thread 1 bead through each and then keep in place with a second knot and burn ends. Cut and burn ends of other 4 strings. Slide the central part of the bracelet until wide enough to wear and close it around your wrist simply by pulling on the 2 beads.

Leaf magic

A classic macramé bracelet, one of the most well-known patterns, always beautiful and stylish: easy to wear and perfect for giving a special touch to any kind of look.

Material needed for the bracelet

▶ Magenta macramé twine, .5mm thick

▶ Frosted turquoise 11/0 seed beads

▶ Frosted dark turquoise 11/0 seed beads

▶ Green fastening bead, approx. 1cm in diameter

... some advice

The same bracelet may be made in less time by not inserting the beads and leaving the strings uncovered at the sides.

Cut 4 strings with a length of 63 in. and 1 string with a length of 74⁴/5 in. Fold in half and make a loop as explained in the tutorial on page 15. Insert 1 holding cord through the loop and secure it to the macramé board, thus dividing the strings into 2 groups of 5 strings each.

1 • Begin by working on the left half of the bracelet. Take the first string on the left and make 1 half knot on the next string, going from left to right.

2 • Knot the same string on the following 4 strings, going from left to right.

3 • Repeat the same steps from right to left in a symmetrical manner.

4 • Knot the 2 strings in the middle, always using the half knot.

5 • Proceed once again on the left half of the bracelet. Take the fourth string on the left and knot it on the fifth string.

... *trivia!*

If you're working on a cushion instead of a rigid board, then you can block your work by using pins.

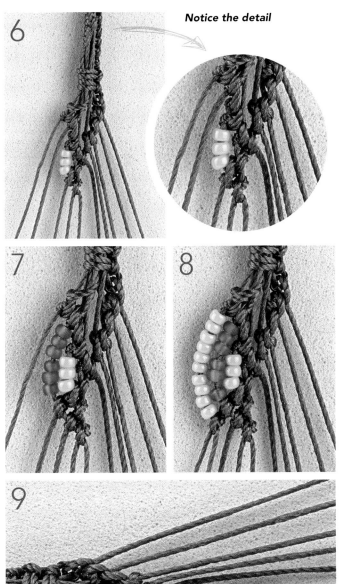

Notice the detail

6 • Take the third string from the left, thread 3 seed beads and knot it on the fourth and on the fifth.

7 • Take the second string from the left, thread 6 seed beads and knot it on the third, fourth and fifth.

8 • Take the first string from the left, thread 10 seed beads and knot it on the second.

9 • Knot the same string on the third, fourth and fifth string.

You've made half a leaf... Great work!

10 • Repeat the same steps on the right half of the bracelet, going from right to left.

11 • Knot together the 2 strings in the middle.

12 • Make another 10 leaf modules in the same way, or even more if desired, depending on your wrist measurement.

... *warning!*

The number of modules to be made varies according to wrist measurements.

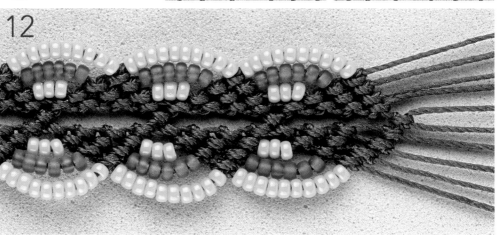

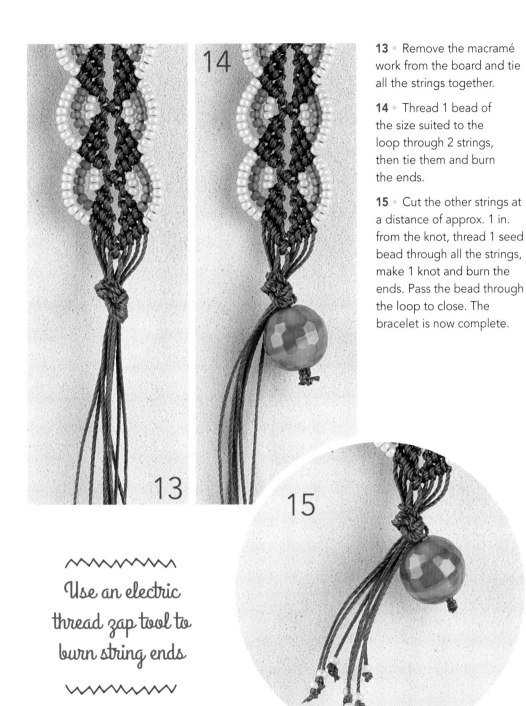

13 • Remove the macramé work from the board and tie all the strings together.

14 • Thread 1 bead of the size suited to the loop through 2 strings, then tie them and burn the ends.

15 • Cut the other strings at a distance of approx. 1 in. from the knot, thread 1 seed bead through all the strings, make 1 knot and burn the ends. Pass the bead through the loop to close. The bracelet is now complete.

Use an electric thread zap tool to burn string ends

Leaf-shaped earrings

Perfect when coupled with its coordinated "Leaf Magic"
bracelet or when worn alone, these light, colorful
and summery earrings are the right frame for any facial shape.

Material needed for the earrings

▶ Magenta macramé twine,
.5mm thick

▶ Opaque turquoise 11/0 seed beads

▶ Frosted turquoise
11/0 seed beads

▶ 2 multifaceted crystals, 7 x 5mm

▶ 2 silver earring clasps

... some advice

*Make the same earring pattern
by alternating colors that contrast
one another distinctively and you'll see
an entirely different final result!*

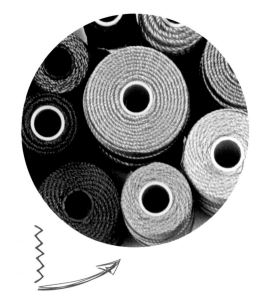

1.

2.

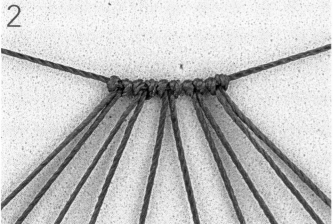

1 • Cut 6 strings with a length of 19³/4 in. Take 1 string, fold in half and using a lark's head knot hitch it onto a holding cord (one of the 6 you will be starting with) secured on the macramé board.

2 • Secure the other 4 strings in the same way and fan them out.

3 • Work on the left half of the earring. Take the second string from the middle towards the left and make 1 half knot on the string next to it on the right. Take the third string, thread 3 seed beads through it and knot it to the next 2 strings, going from left to right. Take the fourth string, thread 5 seed beads through it and knot it to the next 3 strings, going from left to right. Take the fifth string, thread 8 seed beads through it and knot it to the next 4 strings, going from left to right.

4 • Repeat the same steps, in a symmetrical way, in the right half of the earring, going from right to left. Knot the 2 strings in the middle.

5 • Make a second leaf in the same manner. Take the string at the far left and knot it on the 4 following strings, going from left to right. Take the string at the far right and knot it on the 4 following strings, going from right to left. Knot the 2 strings in the middle.

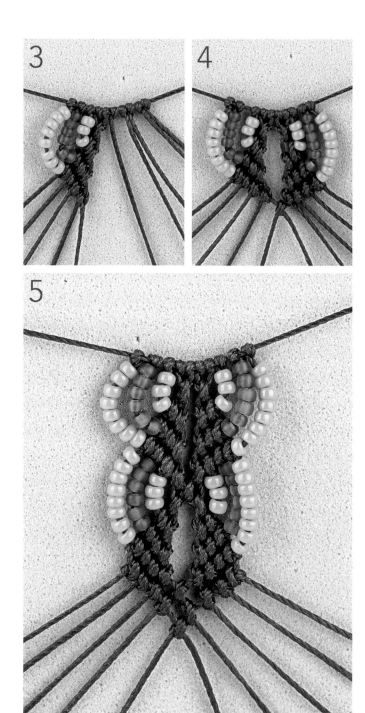

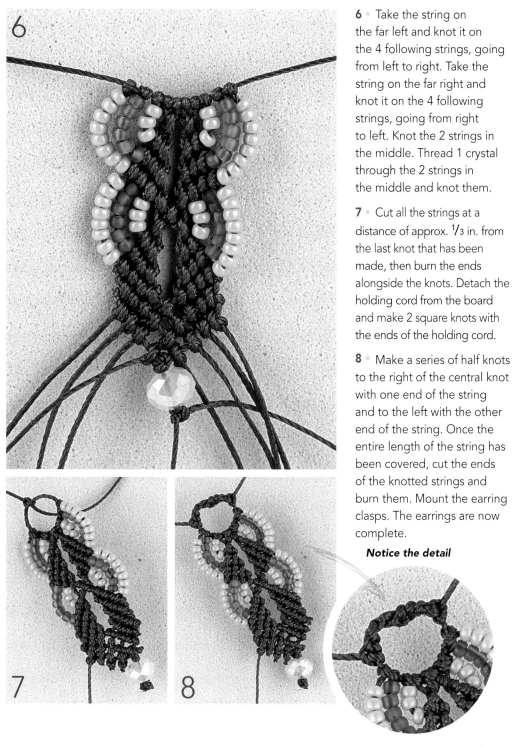

6 Take the string on the far left and knot it on the 4 following strings, going from left to right. Take the string on the far right and knot it on the 4 following strings, going from right to left. Knot the 2 strings in the middle. Thread 1 crystal through the 2 strings in the middle and knot them.

7 Cut all the strings at a distance of approx. $1/3$ in. from the last knot that has been made, then burn the ends alongside the knots. Detach the holding cord from the board and make 2 square knots with the ends of the holding cord.

8 Make a series of half knots to the right of the central knot with one end of the string and to the left with the other end of the string. Once the entire length of the string has been covered, cut the ends of the knotted strings and burn them. Mount the earring clasps. The earrings are now complete.

Notice the detail

A thousand blue waves

A refined and elegant pattern, a sequence of waves
that will wrap around your wrist like lace …
A precious jewel, just the right thing for a special evening.

Material needed for the bracelet

▶ Blue macramé twine,
.5mm thick

▶ Silver 11/0 seed beads

▶ Pearly white 11/0 seed beads

▶ Blue ring-shaped crystals, 3 x 4mm

▶ Blue drop-shaped fastening bead,
1.5 x .9mm

Cut 4 strings with a length of 63 in. and 1 string
with a length of 75 in. Fold in half and make a loop, as
explained in the tutorial on page 15. Insert 1 holding
cord inside the loop and secure it to the macramé
board, fanning all the strings out towards the bottom.
Take 1 string and secure it diagonally to
the left. This will be your holding cord.

1 • Take the first string on the
right and make 1 half knot on
the holding cord.

2 • Knot all the other strings on the holding cord, going from right to left.

3 • Take what has become the first string on the right and secure it diagonally to the left, knot all the underlying strings again on this second holding cord.

4 • Take the second holding cord and secure it diagonally on the right. Knot the first string on the left of the fan on the holding cord and repeat this with the second string, going from left to right.

5 • Take the third string, thread 3 seed beads through it and knot it on the holding cord.

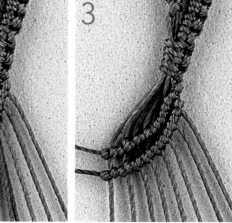

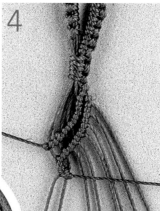

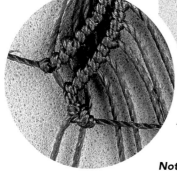

A refined intertwining of shiny beads and crystals

Notice the detail

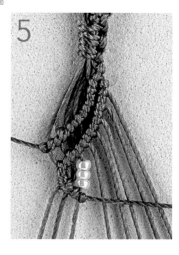

... warning!

The holding cords are always the same: the more internal one is arranged diagonally in front of the fanned-out strings; the more external one should be lightly secured to the top left in order to keep the work pulled taut.

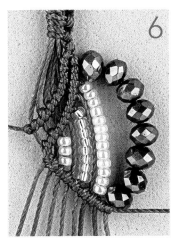

6 • Knot the fourth string on the holding cord. Thread 8 seed beads through the fifth string and knot it onto the holding cord; knot the sixth string, as well. Thread 12 seed beads through the seventh string and knot it onto the holding cord. Thread 8 beads through the eighth string and knot it onto the holding cord.

7 • Thread 3 seed beads onto the first holding cord, then arrange it diagonally to the right immediately below the previous one. Knot all the underlying strings on the holding cord, going from right to left.

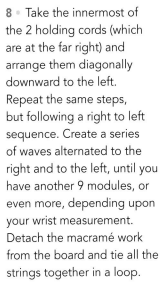

8 • Take the innermost of the 2 holding cords (which are at the far right) and arrange them diagonally downward to the left. Repeat the same steps, but following a right to left sequence. Create a series of waves alternated to the right and to the left, until you have another 9 modules, or even more, depending upon your wrist measurement. Detach the macramé work from the board and tie all the strings together in a loop.

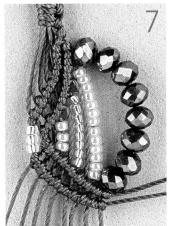

9 • Thread 1 bead (large enough to remain blocked in the loop) through 2 strings, then make 1 knot to block it. Cut the other strings to a measurement of approx. 1³⁄₁₆ in. in length, thread 1 crystal through each one of them and make a knot. Burn the ends of all the strings. Pull the bead through the loop to secure it. The bracelet is now complete.

Wave-shaped earrings

The ideal drop earrings to wear along with the
"Thousand Blue Waves" bracelet. Highlighting them
with a gathered-up hairdo or softly framed by a cascade of curls,
these earrings make one's features shine bright.

Material needed for the earrings

▶ Blue macramé twine,
.5mm thick

▶ Silver 11/0 seed beads

▶ Pearl blue 11/0 seed beads

▶ Blue ring-shaped crystals, 3 x 4mm

▶ 2 silver earring clasps

... some advice

*To secure the strings on the macramé board
in the best way possible, especially if this is lacking
grooves on its edges, you can even use pins
or scotch tape.*

1 • Cut 6 strings with a
length of 20 in. Fold
1 string in half and hitch it
onto a holding cord (one of
the 6) secured with 1 lark's
head knot onto the macramé
board.

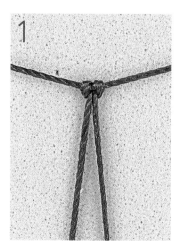

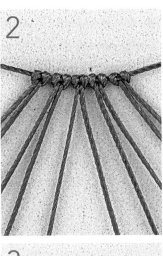

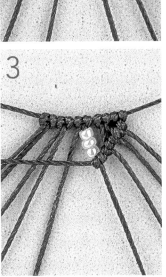

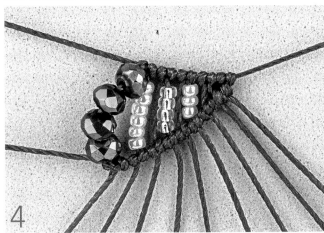

2 • Secure the other 4 strings in the same manner.

3 • Take the string on the far right and secure it to the left diagonally—this will be your first holding cord. Take the second string from the right towards the left and make 1 half knot on the holding cord. Take the third string from the right and knot it to the holding cord. Take the fourth string from the right, thread 3 seed beads through it and knot it on the holding cord.

4 • Take the fifth string from right and knot it on the holding cord. Take the sixth string from right, thread 4 seed beads and knot it on the holding cord. Take the seventh string from right and knot it on the holding cord. Take the eighth string from right, thread 6 seed beads and knot it on the holding cord. Take the ninth string from right, thread 4 crystals and knot it on the holding cord.

5 • Detach the holding cord from the board and make 2 square knots with the ends of the holding cord.

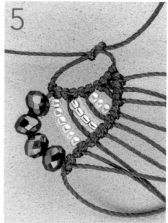

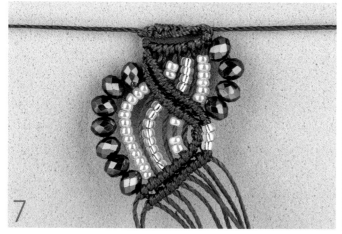

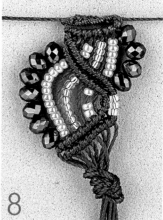

6 • Make a series of half knots to the right of the central knot with one end of the string and to the left with the other end, until a whole loop has been completed. Then secure the two ends to the board again.

7 • Make a wave on the opposite side by following the instructions provided for

"A thousand blue waves" bracelet. Take the first string from the right, the new holding cord, secure it diagonally to the left and knot all the underlying strings on the holding cord.

8 • Detach all the strings from the board and knot them together. Cut at a distance of approx. 1½ in. from the knot that gathers them together.

9 • Thread 1 crystal bead through every string and make 1 knot at approx. ⅓ in. from the end of the string to block the crystal bead, therefore burn the ends of the string. Detach the holding cord from the board. Cut the ends of the tied strings and burn them. Mount the clasps. The earrings are now complete.

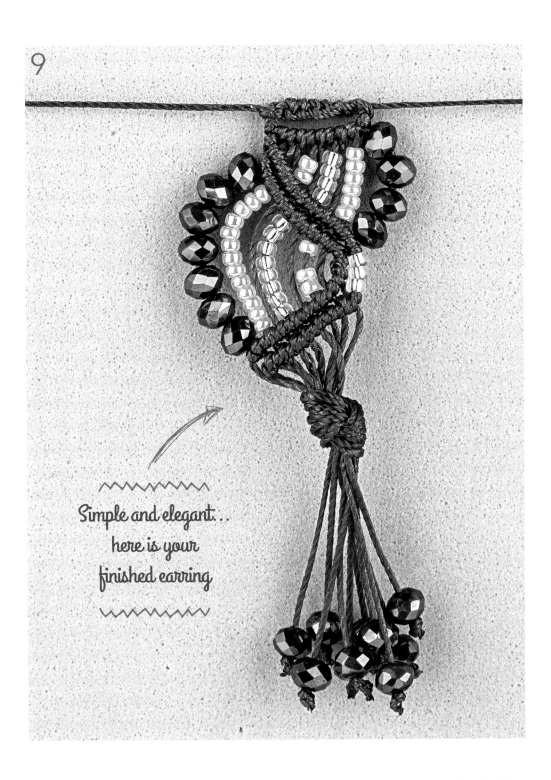

Simple and elegant…
here is your
finished earring

Donut bracelet

An ethnic touch in this bracelet gives another rendition of the leaf motif by enriching it with new elements, like the central one and the large beads in semiprecious stone that give your piece of jewelry that extra special touch.

Material needed for the bracelet

▶ Pink macramé twine, .5mm thick

▶ Turquoise ring-shaped crystals, 3 x 3mm

▶ Emerald green 11/0 seed beads

▶ Light green semiprecious stone beads, 8mm in diameter

▶ Donut in polymer clay (imitation jade) or in stone, approx. 35mm diameter

▶ Green drop crystal bead, approx. 10 x 8mm

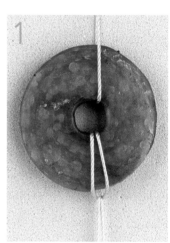

1 • Cut 5 strings with a length of 33½ in. Secure the donut to the macramé board with 1 holding cord: should it have a decorated side, keep the side that will be used as the flip side of the bracelet on top. Secure 1 string in the middle of the donut bead with 1 lark's head knot.

2 • Secure the other 4 strings to the donut bead, again using 1 lark's head knot, and fan them all out towards the bottom.

3 • Knot the 2 central strings. Knot the fourth string from the left to the fifth, then repeat the same procedure in a symmetrical manner on the right.

4 • Take the third string from the left, thread 2 seed beads

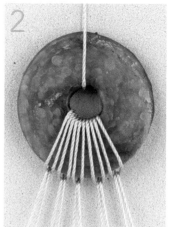

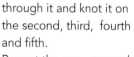

through it and knot it on the fourth and fifth. Repeat the same procedure in a symmetrical manner on the right.

5 • Take the second string on the left and knot it on the third, fourth and fifth. Take the first string from the left, thread 2 crystals

through it and knot it on the second, third, fourth and fifth.
Repeat the same procedure in a symmetrical manner on the right.

6 • Thread 1 light green semiprecious stone bead measuring 8mm through the 2 central strings and knot the fourth string from the left onto the fifth, immediately under the bead.

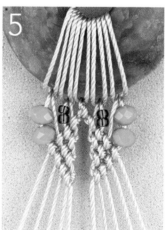

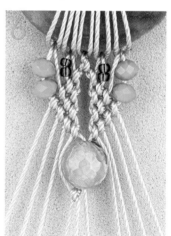

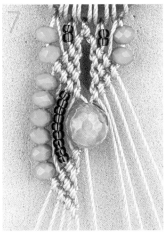

7 • Take the third string from the left, thread 5 seed beads through it and knot it on the fourth and fifth. Take the second string from the left and knot it on the third, fourth and fifth. Take the first string from the left, thread 6 crystals through it and knot it on the second, third, fourth and fifth.

8 • Repeat the same procedure in a symmetrical manner on the right half of the bracelet, going from right to left. Thread 1 bead measuring 8mm through the 2 central strings.

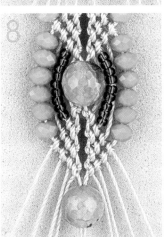

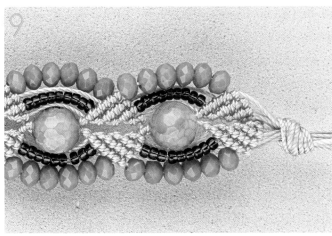

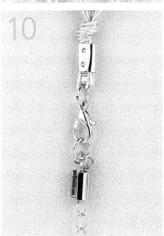

9 • Make another leaf module in the same manner, or even 2, depending upon your wrist measurement. Bear in mind that you have made half the bracelet and that you will have to make as many modules on the opposite side of the donut. Detach the bracelet from the board, turn it towards the right side of the donut and knot all the strings together.

10 • Block all the strings together with metal snap fasteners, cut the excess part of the strings and burn the ends. Do the same thing on both sides of the bracelet. Secure the fastener to the clasp and to the adjustable links using connecting rings.

Infinity waves

A bracelet with a simple design that never goes out of fashion, made using one of the most classic macramé motifs.

Material needed for the bracelet

▶ Pink macramé twine, .5mm thick

▶ Green ring-shaped crystals, 5 x 7mm

▶ Green drop crystal bead, approx. 10 x 8mm

1 • Cut 5 strings with a length of 63 in. Fold in half and make a loop as explained in the tutorial on page 15. Insert the holding cord in the loop and secure it to the macramé board, then divide the strings in 2 groups of 5. Take the 2 central strings and secure them on the upper right and on the upper left. Begin by working on the left half of the bracelet. Take the second string from the middle towards the left and make 1 half knot around the first string. This will be your holding cord.

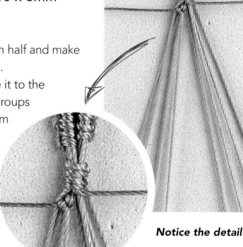

Notice the detail

2 • Take the third string and make 1 half knot around the first string. Repeat the same procedure for the fourth and fifth strings.

3 • Repeat the same steps on the right side, in a symmetrical manner.

4 • Take the fourth string (of the fanned out ones) from the left and secure it on the top left. This will be

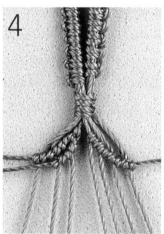

your second holding cord. As for the previous string, knot the first two strings in sequence, from right to left, with a half knot on the holding cord.

5 • Repeat the same steps with the strings going from the middle towards the right, in a symmetrical manner.

6 • Thread 1 crystal through the 2 strings that are now in the middle of your work. Of the 2 strings secured above, take the innermost one and fix it diagonally below to the right, going around the crystal bead. This will be your holding cord.

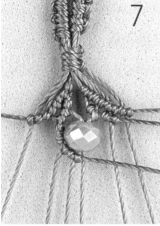

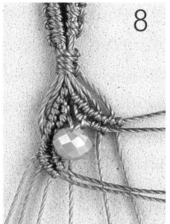

7 • Going from left to right, knot the 2 strings below to the holding cord using a half knot.

8 • Take the first string at the upper left, lead it down diagonally to the bottom right, immediately below the previous one, then proceed as before, knotting the 3 underlying strings onto it.

9 • Repeat the same process going from right to left, in a symmetrical manner.

10 • Bring all the strings downward, take the fifth string from the right and fix it diagonally below to the right. This will be your holding cord. Knot all the 5 underlying strings (on the right) on the holding cord with a half knot, going from left to right.

11 • Take the fourth string from the right and lead it down diagonally right, immediately below the previous one. Then knot the other 5 strings on this one, proceeding as before from left to right.

… some advice

This bracelet may be enriched by changing the central beads, or by adding more beads to the sides. Even the type of fastening chosen may contribute towards changing the final effects.

12 • Take the fourth string from the left and secure it to the top left. This will be your holding cord. Knot the 3 underlying strings on the holding cord, going from right to left.

13 • Take the fourth string from the left and secure it to the top left, immediately below the previous one.

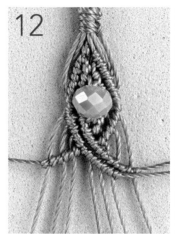

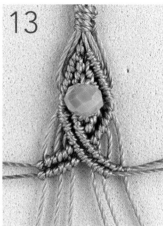

Small crystal beads set in wave motifs

This will be your holding cord. Knot the 3 underlying strings onto the holding cord, proceeding in a sequence from right to left.

14 • Repeat the same steps as before, beginning by threading a crystal bead through the 2 central strings, starting with the right side.

15 • Repeat the same steps on the left side.

16 • Cross the wave motif again and repeat 7 or more times, depending upon your wrist measurement.

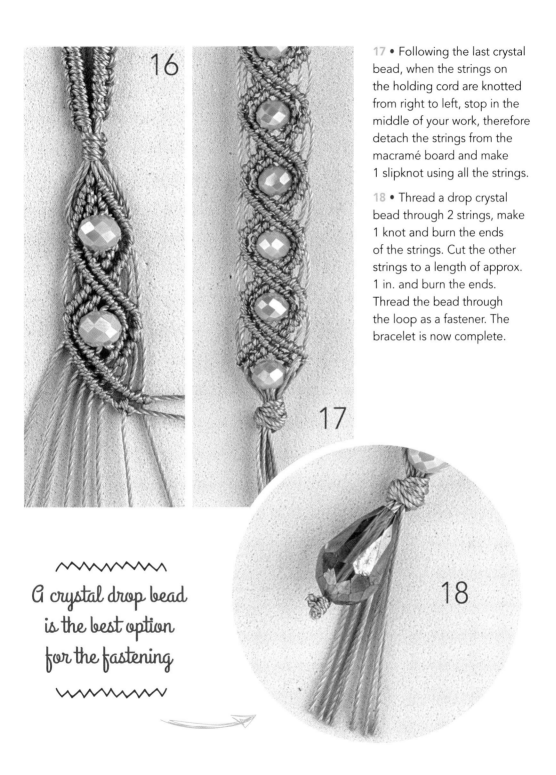

17 • Following the last crystal bead, when the strings on the holding cord are knotted from right to left, stop in the middle of your work, therefore detach the strings from the macramé board and make 1 slipknot using all the strings.

18 • Thread a drop crystal bead through 2 strings, make 1 knot and burn the ends of the strings. Cut the other strings to a length of approx. 1 in. and burn the ends. Thread the bead through the loop as a fastener. The bracelet is now complete.

A crystal drop bead is the best option for the fastening

Drop earrings

To illuminate your face and your smile, choose multifaceted crystal drop beads in your favorite colors. Their macramé setting will make them all the more precious.

Material needed for the earrings

▶ Light green macramé twine, .5mm thick

▶ 2 emerald green crystal briolettes

▶ 2 round multifaceted gray crystals, 6mm in diameter

▶ 2 silver earring clasps

.... trivia! !

A briolette is characterized by small rhombus-shaped faceting.

1 • Cut 5 strings with a length of 23½ in. Take 1 of these strings, thread it through the briolette and tie 1 knot in the middle of the string. Secure the string horizontally on the board, pass holding cord in the space between the first knot and the briolette. Secure this string vertically on the board.

*All the charm
of the East
in this
briolette pendant*

2 • Fold the other strings in half and hitch them onto the first holding cord, using 1 lark's head knot for each one of them.

3 • Take 2 strings in the middle and make 1 half knot.

4 • Take the third string from the left and knot it onto the string to its right.

5 • Do the same on the right (in a symmetrical manner).

6 • Knot the 2 strings in the middle.

7 • Take the second string from the right and knot it onto the first string to its left and then onto the second. Do the same on the right (in a symmetrical manner). Knot the 2 strings in the middle.

8 • Take the third string from the right and knot it onto the first string to its right and then onto the second. Do the same on the left (in a symmetrical manner). Knot the 2 strings in the middle.

9 • Take the end of the first string on the left of your macramé work, previously secured horizontally to the board, and block it diagonally on the bottom right.

10 • Knot the first 4 strings from left to right onto this holding cord.

11 • Do the same, in a symmetrical manner, from right to left. Knot the 2 strings in the middle.

12 • Thread 1 round crystal bead through the 2 strings in the middle. Take the string immediately to the left of the crystal bead and knot it onto the string that is threaded through the crystal bead on the left.

You can make the same object using brighter colors

13 • Working on the left side of the earring, take the first of the 3 free strings to the left and make a series of half knots on the other 2 strings: a spiral will be created.

14 • Continue with the spiral motif for approx. ²/₃ in., until reaching underneath the crystal bead.

15 • Do the same on the right side of the earring, in a symmetrical manner.

… some advice

We suggest using C-Lon twine since it is particularly suited for micro-macramé.

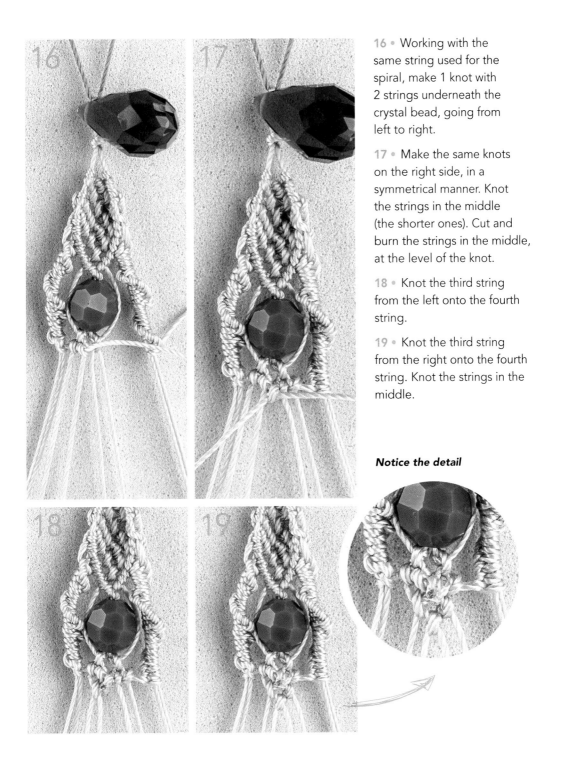

16 • Working with the same string used for the spiral, make 1 knot with 2 strings underneath the crystal bead, going from left to right.

17 • Make the same knots on the right side, in a symmetrical manner. Knot the strings in the middle (the shorter ones). Cut and burn the strings in the middle, at the level of the knot.

18 • Knot the third string from the left onto the fourth string.

19 • Knot the third string from the right onto the fourth string. Knot the strings in the middle.

Notice the detail

You can try using string in contrasting colors ...

20 • Take the second string from the left and knot it onto the third and fourth.

21 • Make the same knots on the right, in a symmetrical manner.

22 • Knot the strings in the middle.

23 • Take the first string on the left and secure it to the bottom right. Knot the second string onto this new holding cord.

24 • Also knot the other 2 strings onto the holding cord.

25 • Repeat the same procedure in a symmetrical way on the right side. Knot the holding cords in the middle. Make a small loop with the 2 strings in the middle, making another overhand knot.

26 • Cut and burn the ends of all the strings. Remove the earring from the macramé board and cut the holding cord, turn the earring upside-down so that the briolette remains hanging. Mount the earring clasps in the upper loop. The earrings are now complete.

Ethnic earrings

In these pendant earrings, the open part
in the middle dominates over the rest, making them
quite visible yet not excessively heavy.

Material needed for the earrings

▶ Green macramé twine,
.5mm thick

▶ 2 beads, 6mm in diameter

▶ Ring-shaped crystal beads, 3 x 4mm

▶ 2 silver earring clasps

... some advice

{ *When decorating these earrings, you can use different
types of beads instead of the ring-shaped crystals:
round, oval, drop, cubic, cone-shaped, double cone-
shaped, rhombus-shaped... unleash your imagination!* }

1 • Cut 6 strings with a
length of 19¾ in., secure 1
horizontally on the macramé
board (holding cord), fold the
second one in half and hitch
it onto the holding cord using
1 lark's head knot.

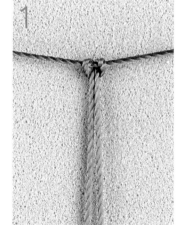

2 • Hitch the other 4 strings to the holding cord in the same way and fan them out.

3 • Take the 2 strings in the middle, make 1 half knot, thread through 1 bead measuring 6mm. Knot the fourth string from the left to the third.

4 • Continue by also knotting what was the fourth string even to the second and first, going from right to left.

5 • Make the same knots in a symmetrical manner on the other side of the bead.

6 • Take the first string from the left and secure it diagonally on the bottom right.

7 • Knot the first 4 strings from the left towards the right on the holding cord.

8 • Make the same knots to the right, in a symmetrical manner.

Notice the detail

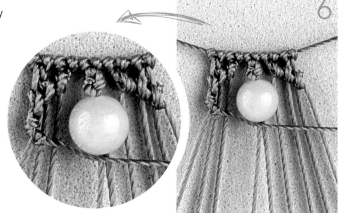

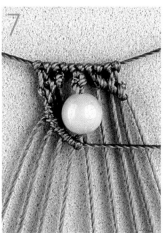

9 • Knot together the 2 holding cords that can now be found in the middle and then secure them taut on the upper right and on the upper left.

10 • Knot all the underlying strings onto the holding cords, going from the middle to the left.

Two simple earrings of ethnic charm

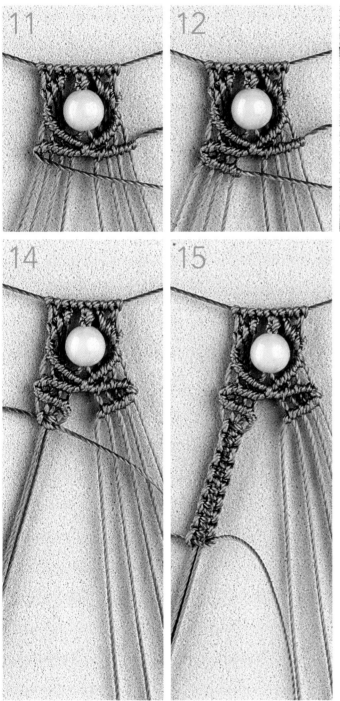

11 • Make the same knots in a symmetrical manner, going from the middle to the right. Take the holding cord on the left and position it on the bottom right.

12 • Knot the 4 underlying strings from the left to the right.

13 • Make the same knots, in a symmetrical manner, from right to left.

14 • Make a series of 9 square knots with the first 5 strings of the macramé work.

15 • To make the square knots, take the first and fifth string from left to right—these will be used as knotting cords—and add the second, third and fourth strings to the middle.

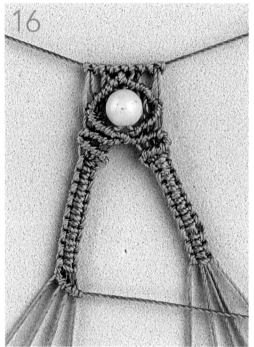

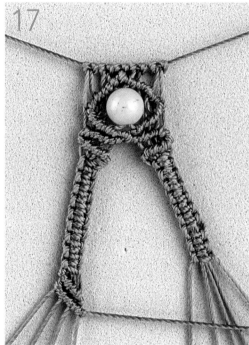

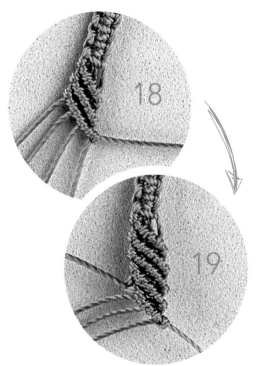

16 • Make the same knots on the right side of the earring. Take the first string to the left and secure it diagonally on the bottom right. Knot the underlying 4 strings onto this holding cord.

17 • Bring the holding cord down, select the string that is now the first one to the left, secure it to the bottom right and, as before, knot the underlying 4 strings onto this holding cord.

18 • Repeat the same procedure a third time.

19 • Repeat the same procedure again for a fourth and fifth time.

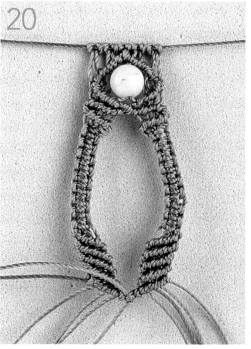

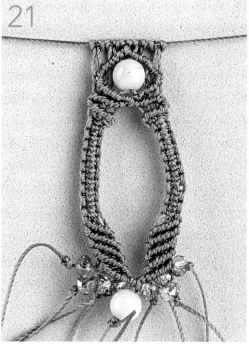

20 • Repeat the same knots on the right side. Knot 2 holding cords in the middle.

21 • Thread 1 bead through the 2 central strings and knot together once again. Thread 1 small crystal bead on each of the 8 strings that emerge from the macramé work, then block these crystal beads as close as possible to the piecework with some small knots.

22 • Cut the ends of the strings and burn them. Detach the macramé work from the board and make 1 knot between the ends of the holding cord. Make a series of half knots in the top arch of the holding cord; cut the excess parts and burn the ends. Mount the earring clasps. The earrings are now complete.

Ethnic cabochon

A rich and special type of bracelet, this alone is enough to make a fashion statement: all you have to do to highlight its beauty is wear it with a basic simple sweater. Extend the ends and you will come up with a marvelous necklace.

Material needed for the bracelet

▶ Black macramé twine, .5mm thick

▶ Turquoise ring-shaped crystal beads, 3 x 4mm

▶ Red 11/0 seed beads

▶ Red cube-shaped bead, 4mm

▶ Turquoise ring-shaped crystal beads, 5 x 7mm

▶ Cabochon in polymer clay, 25mm in diameter

▶ Black onyx bead, 10mm in diameter

Make your bracelet all the more precious by adding small crystal leaves

1 • Cut 1 string with a length of 23½ in. and 1 string with a length of 98½ in. These measurements are for a cabochon measuring 20mm in diameter. Fold the shortest string in half and hitch it onto the macramé board. Make a noose on the longer string and fix it alongside the previous one, on the other side of the board.

2 • Take the longer string and knot it with a half knot on the first string to the right of the board, directing the work towards the middle of the 2 strings.

3 • Knot this same string on the second string secured onto the board and make the knot symmetrically to the first knot, so that the work always proceeds towards the middle of the 2 strings.

4 • Proceed the same way, alternating 1 knot from right to left and 1 knot from left to right. Continue until you have a length of approx. 3¾ in.: it should be shaped so that it is slightly smaller than the circumference of the cabochon, then the macramé work may be detached from the board.

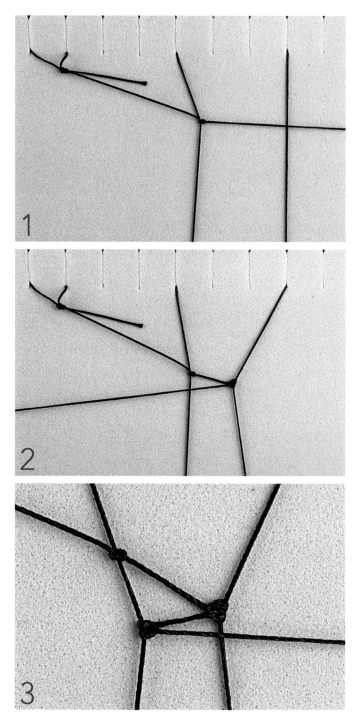

... warning!

It is important to calculate the distance between the 2 strings secured to the board in the proper way. Take into consideration that when the piece becomes narrower in the right way, the distance between the 2 strings is reduced to about one-third of the original distance. The actual distance between the 2 strings is assessed after the first 5 or 6 knots. Also bear in mind that to set a cabochon like the present one, the holding cords must be at a distance of approx. $\frac{1}{3}$ in.: secure them at least 3 notches away from one another on the macramé board (closer distances are used for setting coins or flat discs with a minimum thickness).

4

5 • Cut half of the holding cord and wrap the macramé work around the cabochon. Knot the 4 ends of the 2 holding cords, initially the 2 that close the loop on the back of the cabochon and then the 2 that close the loop on the front of the cabochon. At this point you have 6 strings coming out of the macramé work: divide them into 2 groups of 3 strings and knot them twice tightly between one another, therefore cut and burn the ends. The setting is now complete.

6 • Insert 1 holding cord on the opposite side of the setting.

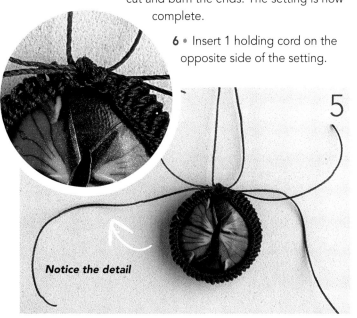

Notice the detail

5

6

Secure it onto the macramé board.

7 • Cut 4 strings with a length of 33½ in. Fold in half and insert between the strings of the cabochon setting. Make a knot onto each couple of strings, then fan out towards the bottom.

8 • Thread 1 square bead through 2 strings and make 1 knot underneath the bead.

9 • Thread 1 square bead through each of the other 3 couples and make 1 knot underneath the bead.

10 • Again, knot the first 2 strings and secure the second from the left horizontally. This is your first holding cord.

11 • Knot all other strings onto the holding cord, from left to right.

The cabochon motif brings to mind a butterfly!

12 • Take the string from the far left and fix it horizontally to the right. This will be the second of your holding cords. Knot all the other strings on the holding cord, going from left to right.

13 • Take the second holding cord (the innermost one) and place it diagonally on the bottom left. Lightly secure the outermost holding cord to the top right in order to keep the work pulled taut. Take the first string on the right among the underlying ones and knot it onto the holding cord.

14 • Take the second string on the right among the underlying ones and knot it onto the holding cord.

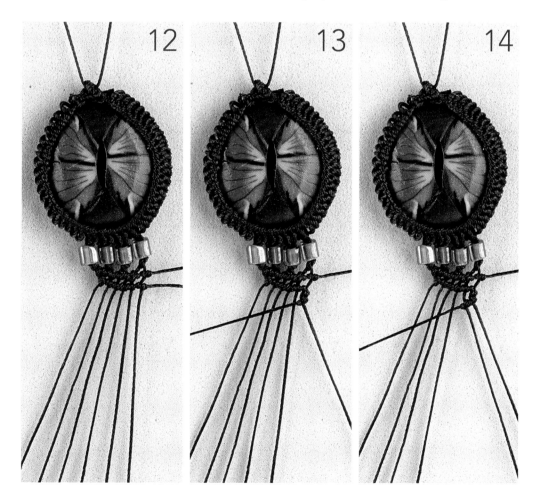

15 • Take the third string from right to left, thread 3 seed beads through it and then knot it onto the holding cord.

16 • Take the fourth string from right to left, thread 5 seed beads through it and then knot it onto the holding cord. Take the fifth string from right to left, thread 7 seed beads through it and then knot it onto the holding cord. Take the sixth string from right to left, thread 1 large crystal bead and 3 small crystal beads onto it, then knot it onto the holding cord.

17 • Thread 1 large crystal through the first holding cord and arrange it diagonally at the bottom left, immediately under the previous holding cord. Knot all the underlying strings on the holding cord, moving from right to left.

18 • Arrange the last holding cord you have worked with diagonally at the bottom right. Moving from left to right, knot the first and second strings on the holding cord. Thread 4 seed beads through the third string, 7 seed beads on the fourth, 9 seed beads on the fifth, 2 small crystal beads, 1 large crystal bead and again 2 small crystal beads on the sixth, then knot them on the holding cord.

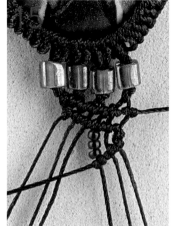

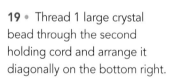

19 • Thread 1 large crystal bead through the second holding cord and arrange it diagonally on the bottom right.

20 • Similarly create (but symmetrically) a wave on the left and then half a wave on the right. The half wave has 0 seed beads on the first 2 strings, 2 seed beads on the third, 3 seed beads on the fourth, 4 seed beads on the fifth and

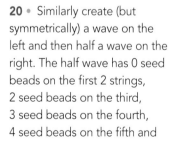

2 small crystal beads on the sixth string. Divide the strings into 2 groups of 4 strings each, then make a series of square knots on the 2 groups of 4 strings (same procedure used for the loop and illustrated on page 15).

21 • Continue with the knots on both sides for approx. $1/3$ in., then knot together using an overhand knot, cut at a length of approx. $1/2$ in. and burn the ends.

22 • Repeat the wave pattern on the other side of the cabochon. At the end of the half wave, tie all the strings together using an overhand knot.

23 • Thread 2 strings through 1 bead that is large enough to block the loop; knot the 2 strings underneath the bead and burn the ends. Cut and burn the ends of all the other strings. The bracelet is now complete.

Diana Crialesi, architect, is a professional crafter who has run an artistic craftsmanship workshop since 2006. She creates jewels and accessories using various techniques: polymer clays, macramé, soutache and wire wrapping; she also conducts courses on these techniques and tutorials in partnership with YouTube on channel Archidee (www.youtube.com/archideedidiana – www.archideeonline.com – www.facebook.com/diana.archidee).

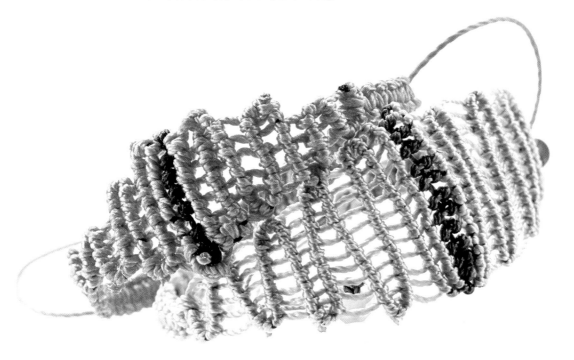